Have You Seen This Hamster?

Level 8 - Purple

Helpful Hints for Reading at Home

The graphemes (written letters) and phonemes (units of sound) used throughout this series are aligned with Letters and Sounds. This offers a consistent approach to learning whether reading at home or in the classroom.

HERE IS A LIST OF PHONEMES FOR THIS PHASE OF LEARNING. AN EXAMPLE OF THE PRONUNCIATION CAN BE FOUND IN BRACKETS.

Phase 5			
ay (day)	ou (out)	ie (tie)	ea (eat)
oy (boy)	ir (girl)	ue (blue)	aw (saw)
wh (when)	ph (photo)	ew (new)	oe (toe)
au (Paul)	a_e (make)	e_e (these)	i_e (like)
o_e (home)	u_e (rule)		

Phase 5 Alternative Pronunciations of Graphemes			
a (hat, what)	e (bed, she)	i (fin, find)	o (hot, so, other)
u (but, unit)	c (cat, cent)	g (got, giant)	ow (cow, blow)
ie (tied, field)	ea (eat, bread)	er (farmer, herb)	ch (chin, school, chef)
y (yes, by, very)	ou (out, shoulder, could, you)		

HERE ARE SOME WORDS WHICH YOUR CHILD MAY FIND TRICKY.

Phase 5 Tricky Words			
oh	their	people	Mr
Mrs	looked	called	asked
could			

TOP TIPS FOR HELPING YOUR CHILD TO READ:

- Allow children time to break down unfamiliar words into units of sound and then encourage children to string these sounds together to create the word.
- Encourage your child to point out any focus phonics when they are used.
- Read through the book more than once to grow confidence.
- Ask simple questions about the text to assess understanding.
- Encourage children to use illustrations as prompts.

This book focuses on the grapheme /ch/ and is a purple level 8 book band.

Have You Seen This Hamster?

Written by
William Anthony

Illustrated by
Amy Li

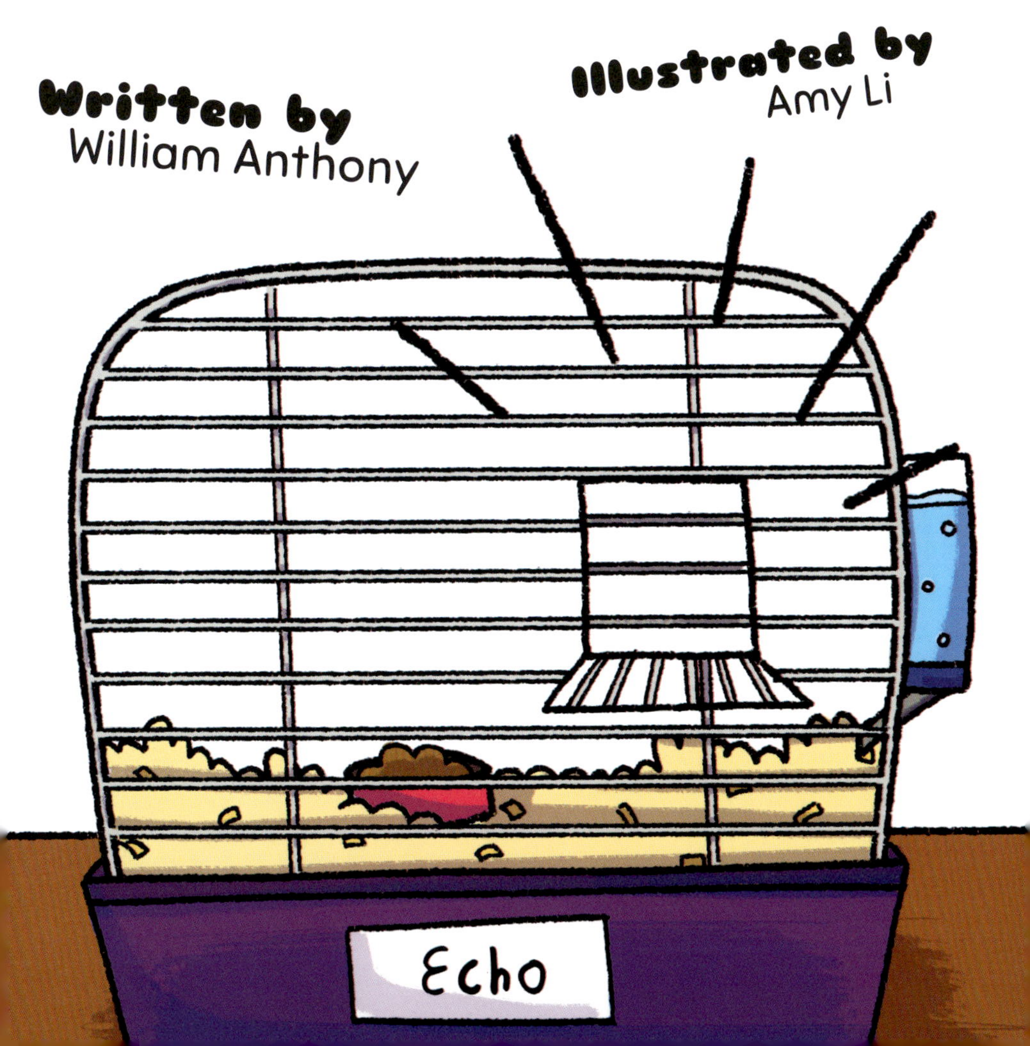

Monday morning is hard. The fun of the weekend is over, and school is back again. Mr Chip was reading out the register. He was the cover teacher while Mrs March was not in.

Zach always dealt with the morning tasks. He made sure all the pens were out and the books were on the desks. He turned on the lights and organised the chairs too.

The best task was to make sure the class hamster, Echo, had food and a drink.
But you cannot feed a hamster that is not in his cage...
This was not good.

"Erm, Mr Chip?" muttered Zach. "Echo's cage is open." Mr Chip's face went pale.
"Is he still in there?" asked Mr Chip in hope.
"Long gone," blubbered Zach. "So is his wheel."

The class gasped. Echo was missing.
Today was bad, and they had not even started maths yet.
Chris and Rochelle gave each other a look.
They had pretended to be detectives at lunch and break times for years.

Now was their time to crack a real case. Mr Chip did not want them to miss lessons. But he did not want Mrs March to find out that Echo was missing even more.

Mr Chip gave Chris and Rochelle a tip.
They needed to talk to the librarian.
The librarian had one headphone in
and was munching on a choc-chip cookie.
"Has a book been borrowed about hamsters?"
asked Rochelle.

The librarian spluttered something past his mouthful. Rochelle's eyes grew wide. Chris' eyes were wider.

"Did he just say the chef took a book called 'How to Cook a Hamster'?" whispered Chris.

Rochelle nodded with fear.

The kitchen door burst open.
"Oi, chef!" yelled Chris. He was fired up now.
Even Rochelle could not hold him back.
"How could you cook Echo? He is just
a helpless hamster!"

Chris was not playing around.
"What scheme are you plotting?"
Chris blurted out, shaking his fist.
"What do you mean?" quivered the chef.
"The book!" said Rochelle. "How to Cook
a Hamster!"
"Oh dear," said the chef.

"You have it all mixed up. The book I took was 'How to Cook a Ham Star'. I could never cook a hamster!" said the chef. He held up his book and showed Chris today's school dinner.

Chris looked at the ground. This was awkward.
"Well... We'll let you off this time," he said.
"But we'll be watching you."
The chef was not the culprit.

In fact, the chef was a good helper, not a thief.
He gave them a clue.
Late last Friday, he had seen the tech teacher in Chris and Rochelle's classroom.
Chris was off again.

Chris burst into the tech room.
"Oi, tech tea–" he started, shaking his fist as Rochelle stopped him in his tracks.

Rochelle took the lead this time.
"Echo is missing," she said to the tech teacher, "and we think you might have been at the place the crime happened."

"I was there," she admitted.
"Aha!" Chris interrupted.
"But I was making Echo a new high-tech wheel! Look!" said the teacher.
The teacher held up a machine that looked like it came from the future.

"Echo was still in his cage when I took his wheel," said the teacher.
It looked like the culprit was not the chef or the tech teacher. Chris and Rochelle were out of clues.

Mr Chip was quite flustered when the kids told him the news.
"Check again," he said. "Mrs March will hate me forever. I feel sick to my stomach!"

Mr Chip bounded off to wipe the sweat from his head.

"What can we do?" wondered Chris.

"You can stop shaking a fist at teachers, for a start," said Rochelle.

"Let's make some 'missing hamster' signs. It's our last hope," said Rochelle with a frown. Chris, Rochelle and the rest of the class attached the posters to walls all over town.

Thursday came with no luck. Friday was no better. No one had seen Echo. Chris and Rochelle had no leads. It was hopeless.

Mr Chip was still quivering under his desk. He did not want Mrs March to catch sight of him after Echo had vanished on his watch. It was time to get past the tragic loss of Echo.

Monday morning rolled around again and Mrs March was back. She bounded into the room with a smile.
The kids were slumped in their chairs.
They looked deflated.

"What happened to make you all look so sad?" asked Mrs March. "I'll help to cheer you up."

Rochelle looked up.

Then she remembered.

Then her cheeks went red.

"Oh no..." she said.

Mrs March held up a small ball of fur wearing a kilt.
A chorus of groans filled the room as the kids remembered Mrs March had been to Scotland... and taken Echo with her.

They put their heads in their hands, their heads on their desks and their coats over their faces.

"What?" said a confused Mrs March.

"What is it?!"

Have You Seen This Hamster?

1. What is Mr Chip's job?

2. What was the school chef cooking?
   - (a) A hamster
   - (b) A ham star
   - (c) Beef

3. Who do you think handled the investigation better – Chris or Rochelle? Why?

4. Where was Echo the whole time?

5. If your class could have a pet, what pet would you choose?

King's Lynn, Norfolk, PE30 4LS, UK

ISBN 978-1-80155-479-4

A catalogue record for this book is available from the British Library.

Have You Seen This Hamster?
Written by William Anthony
Illustrated by Amy Li

An Introduction to BookLife Readers...

Our Readers have been specifically created in line with the London Institute of Education's approach to book banding and are phonetically decodable and ordered to support each phase of the Letters and Sounds document.

Each book has been created to provide the best possible reading and learning experience. Our aim is to share our love of books with children, providing both emerging readers and prolific page-turners with beautiful books that are guaranteed to provoke interest and learning, regardless of ability.

BOOK BAND GRADED using the Institute of Education's approach to levelling.

PHONETICALLY DECODABLE supporting each phase of Letters and Sounds.

EXERCISES AND QUESTIONS to offer reinforcement and to ascertain comprehension.

BEAUTIFULLY ILLUSTRATED to inspire and provoke engagement, providing a variety of styles for the reader to enjoy whilst reading through the series.

AUTHOR INSIGHT: **WILLIAM ANTHONY**

William Anthony's involvement with children's education is quite extensive. He has written a vast array of titles for BookLife Publishing, across a wide range of subjects. William graduated from Cardiff University with a 1st Class BA (Hons) in Journalism, Media and Culture, creating an app and a TV series, among other things, during his time there.

William Anthony has also produced work for the Prince's Trust, a charity created by HRH The Prince of Wales, that helps young people with their professional future. He has created animated videos for a children's education company that works closely with the charity.

This book focuses on the grapheme /ch/ and is a purple level 8 book band.